NAME WITHHELD

Also by Lisa Sewell:

The Way Out

NAME WITHHELD

poems | LISA SEWELL

Four Way Books
New York City

Distributed by
University Press of New England
Hanover and London

Editorial Office
Four Way Books
POB 535, Village Station
New York, NY 10014
www.fourwaybooks.com

Library of Congress Catalogue Card Number: 2004113814

ISBN 1-884800-68-8

Cover art: Alice Oh, detail of "Phases of Conception," no. 42.03. Water base mixed media on canvas, 58" x 67", 2004. By permission of the artist.

Book cover design: Cubanica.

This book is manufactured in the United States of America and printed on acid-free paper.

Four Way Books is a not-for-profit literary press. We are grateful for the assistance we receive from individual donors, government arts agencies and private foundations.

This publication is made possible with public funds from the New York State Council on the Arts, a state agency.

Distributed by University Press of New England
One Court Street, Lebanon, NH 03766

We are a proud member of the Council of Literary Magazines and Presses.

ACKNOWLEDGMENTS

Many thanks to the editors of the following publications and web projects, where some of these poems (or versions of them) first appeared:

American Poetry Review, Denver Quarterly, Electronic Poetry Review, Gulf Coast, The Journal, The Laurel Review, Paris Review, Ploughshares, Quarterly West, The Recorder, third coast, and *Shenandoah.*

"Meteor Shower" appeared in the catalog for *Sarah McEneaney,* curated by Igrid Schaffner, Institute of Contemporary Art, University of Pennsylvania, Philadelphia, January 24-April 24, 2004.

I am also grateful to the National Endowment for the Arts, the Leeway Foundation, the Pennsylvania Council for the Arts, the MacDowell Colony, the Corporation of Yaddo, Fundación Valparaiso, the Tyrone Guthrie Center and the Virginia Center for the Creative Arts for grants and residencies that were crucial to the completion of the manuscript.

Thanks as well, and eternal gratitude, to my editor, Sally Ball, and to Martha Rhodes, for their enthusiasm, care, and support.

Also, Nathalie Anderson, Rick Benjamin, A.V. Christie, Eamon Grennan, Robert Marshall, Valerie Martínez, Claudia Rankine, Vincent Sherry, Elaine Terranova, and Suzanne Wise read and responded to this work at various stages. I thank them for their patience, insight and acts of generosity, editorial and otherwise.

For John

Contents

FOUR

I had a terror—since September—I could tell to none—and so I sing, as the Boy does by the Burying Ground—because I am afraid—.

Emily Dickinson in a letter to T.W. Higginson

ONE

HANDS AND PSALMS

A hand is the terminus of a human arm, thirty-six or more
connected bones and muscles, all designed
for grasping—

it's the thin smattering of applause, what's offered
when you have a little trouble getting off

the ground, though that's not how it seems
to the tourists on the lawn, shielding their eyes

against the glare, and to me, waving back
as though I were visible, or the girl at the Burger King

on the way to Baltimore whose DNA
had skipped the sequences for wrist and limb,

jumping straight to digit, opposable thumb, so her hands
grew directly from the unballed sockets
of her shoulders.

You'd think hands could do so little stranded there
above her ribcage, but they swayed

like living epaulets and held their own wise counsel. Praise
for the hands that do what they are told

is impossible and forbidden, that can smack
a person silly or spread like balm above the angled limbs of grief

and draw the clear stream of disappointment out, to the knuckles
that wedge themselves between muscle and bone
and release the hand

that held too long or squeezed too hard
or not enough

and to the men who wanted me (without consent)
when I was seventeen and wore my green t-shirt

with a yellow number twenty-three
emblazoned on my chest.

Put yourself in my hands, they said, with no *may I put my arm
around your shoulder*, no, *may I stroke the endolateral*

surface of your thigh, and like Mary in her azure hood, I
was lifted bodily toward heaven.

Here is a poem for the chain-link fence at the back of a softball field
in Van Nuys, California, and the hands that did exactly
what we wanted.

Even now, I hear my father among the slender wheat-like weeds,
his yellow leather gloves trying to pull out all the wildness.

He says I'm going to hell in a hand basket, and I wanted that
Didn't I, didn't I?

MY SOLE GENEALOGY

Saul, Solly, Saywell, Seuell, Suhill, Swill—

Derived from several sources, these untamed names
descend from *victory, strength* or an English place
meaning 'seven wells' (not 'sea wall,' as my father claims).

The Domesday book lists a 'gentle man,' the very least
a belted knight, who followed the Black Prince
into Aquitane, and though no place of origin can be proven

we can trace two centuries of landed blood, from Henry (II)
who made his pitch at Newbury, to Reverend Justice Samuel,
the only judge at Salem to publicly acknowledge regrets.

But for a Polish Jew in Chicago, 1938, who fashioned himself
from the blue inscription on the flyleaf of *Crime
and Punishment* or lifted the name from the open mouth

of a bottle blonde or stole it to commemorate a road trip
through Virginia, it seemed Sewell could truly designate
his character and station, erase the unpronounceable history

already wreaking havoc across a newly foreign homeland
with a sound like cruel, like shame. Perhaps he liked
the sibilance, the proximity to jewel and shul,

for he consigned it to sisters, mother, a father who never
gleaned the language well enough to rearrange the past
with an accent on American, and fool the army, customers

and neighbors. Once at a dinner party in London, Ontario,
a blue-blood learned man advised me to look
to my genealogy, as though all origins stare steadily

from a line of aging photographs. Some other name
stuttered behind teeth and lips as I let the fable stay,
claiming signposts in towns from Texas to New Jersey.

Salde, Sooll, Sewilde, Sowl, Swall, Sowel, Sowley, Sold—

And though my tongue slips on first and final
syllables, and I am not well or seaworthy
or the sower of a wild and swelling history,

I can see the shifty underground of Southern
California was a solid place and open chamber
for this sweet and wily, this willful soul a'starting.

In a dream fashioned by collision
California was birthplace to my self,
my sister, and the continent's youngest mountain range.

The San Andreas, like a god that loved us,
followed the coastline from Mendocino to Palm Springs—
and almost everywhere we found suspect terrain:

Point Reyes, our favorite spot on the coast
traveled six hundred feet northwest in 1906, and the sturdy
single span of Golden Gate swings wildly in the movies
when the big one finally strikes.

No one knows which fold of frontal lobe
writes the signal or what the matter is.

Perhaps a scar from an early undocumented fall
or breach birth, breach of contract, being tossed
into the breach like a ball.

Fault zone, fault line, fault trace, fault branch.
Though the brain sits protected in its vault
many faults, termed blind, do not break the surface.

But the earthquake is not unseen or sightless.

Try not to look up. Protect your head.
Stay in if you are in, and outside if you are out.

Despite charges of insouciance, many Californians worry
for the future, the always something concealed:

a Druid king in the peat bog, a birthmark on the brain,
the movement of air in subterrestrial chambers,
an agitation of the sea.

A mother tends to shoulder blame. Imagine my eyes
blurred, my skin rubbed red where cheek and chin had met
and met, a mother's question: *Where have you been?*

The four turtles that carry the world argue and fight
swimming off in four directions.

The argument glides beneath the surface,
floats the broken-bottle vinegar smell
and early morning, the chimney refuses.

In the moderate quake, when plates diverge
the seismic waves cause land to quiver.
The crust may bend, then crack.

The girl in her nightgown rushes downstairs.
She too wants to flee the country, to drop and cover—
though weren't we a family then?

Now everything in the book of junctures
asks how to endure the landscape after uplift.

And I thought to my dream
the man looks a fright
pale as death, pale and white.

I put my head against stone to stop the vertigo,
made stop and go, let him, let me.

Both of us know Jimmy Stewart,
afraid as he tails Kim Novak, not heroic but obsessed
scaling the vertiginous depths of San Francisco.

When the argument subsides
a girl might be detached *and* uplifted
might buoyantly rise, a plume or hotspot

like the red and black profiles of Mounts Dana
and Kaweah. A fault is gritty, shattered, unmappable

as folds of envy on the brain's gray corridors.
A photograph of the crust beneath L.A. reminds you
of a car window smashed by a baseball.

She was the same woman, only different,
wearing better clothes and blonder hair, a secret.

And a girl like me, tilted to the West,
some of the same genes shaping her height
and disposition, falling not asleep

but atremor, bruised where her cheek grazed the floorboards.

Anything ruined or broken could not be helped—
her *grand mal* undoing poised between
epigram and epiphany.

Where was the earthquake? What is a fault?
What did it feel like? How many earthquakes
happen each year? Every month?
Day? Minute?

In the twenty-first century we can map
the shifting impulse but what moves remains unclear:

my sister wakes from a nap she did not take,
her jaw stiff, her tongue quiet
beneath the fingers of the bus driver.

The neurologist speculates.
Why and when remain a mystery.

The blonde never fell or died—
it was a trick of emotion, a burst of the eye.

And that too earthly rumble in the distance:
one of the eight mighty elephants that hold up the land,
grown weary, has lowered its head.

Name Withheld

What one felt first of all, felt real (the gasping
for breath) and unreal (the park's dim corridor),
likely (what she knew she knew
always) and unjust, but nothing like script
or the speech of confession: not *I*
was filled with dread, but redress churning,
not *a panic attack*, but burning burning.

Two turned into the park at midnight
to cut through, avoid traffic—not turned
as in became a frog or ghoul, and yet
with that turn, one became a monster
of neglect and one fell into a dream
from which I would only partially resume.

To cut through was the logical course
agreed to by both, but as one rode ahead
the other was left well enough adrone
in the dark with murder in mind
and a fear that mid-wifed the birth
of desire in the one and the death
in the other, for if *yes* means *no* doesn't *stop*
mean *yes, let's go, let go, go ahead.*

Alone in the dark with marauders
around the bend, though unseen and
unheard—both knew about, had viewed
the woman, *name withheld*, caught
behind the tree by the camera's eye,
frantic to hide what the videotape revealed—
one continued instead of turning back
or away (couldn't the woman have stayed
in bed?) from the curved future, dark bend
where the deserter waited in the ardor
of guilt and panic (whose?)

I continued instead of turning
from the arbor of lick, lips whose kiss
would spell out apology but not dispel
the hurt I chose and didn't choose,
though the woman in the park was made
to see what she had been through, forced to be
the woman sobbing on TV *stop them,*
stop, shying from the lens that held her
fast and the stranger observing
from the piracy of a private living room.

I chose and didn't choose the only link
between us—the one caught, the other
riding—which was the park, or the park,
these sentences, and a wounding
I cannot name or see. This is not a public
tale. This is privacy in action.

We did choose but were chosen.
We did not freeze (it was a humid night in
June) and are forever frozen on trial
and the wrong trail with our blindness
faced toward the camera's eye. Only
the syllables of accident to shield
and conceive us: *I tried to hide*
from the lens. I couldn't stop.

NESTING CLAUSE

Because every pond must have its great blue heron and we swam in
the cold June (without pleasure) to exercise our hearts

Whether a crane means good luck and prosperity as in the Genji
tale or faith in God or faithlessness or purity

If I'd had a little more in him some faith more listening more
listing in his direction more echolocation

As the hornbill walls herself inside a nest-hole with mud and dung
leaving only a crack through which the male feeds her

Though by then my love had grown paltry having fed on nothing
so long nothing more or less would appease it

Because even the crawl even the breaststroke and butterfly could
not warm us

Because now the pearl of great price I seek on the innermost
and highest shelf (the lip of the question the bead) and he has
pledged his troth as in an ancient tale to another

Though she spoke in my dream first in a rapid stream of Japanese
rapt and breathless with joy or its opposite then the broken
feminine translation

Whether she with her foreign tongue could better aim better
narrow the beam to the place that would make his heart break
or break open

If my bones were hollowed or honeycombed or molded into thin
curved plates and compassion were (not) the same as passion

As the sex shy avocets channel their drives into preening (for the
  male) or bill-dipping (for the female) before progressing to
  coition

Because I wanted her to say *bye-bye sayonara* long before I woke
  and wanted him not to be so well proportioned and photogenic

Because the East African male weaver (golden or Clarke's) works
  hard from dawn to dusk and the female supervises from nearby
  sometimes inspecting

Whether calling out I called harm back into my path the bruising
  so close at hand walking toward me then with his head down

If I sit at my computer barefoot ungrounded and the small
  electrical shocks are like something very sharp (a tongue) or
  hot (a needle)

Like mourning or melancholia where the object lost has not
  perhaps actually died we regard it as just to call the temper of
  grief *painful*

Though maybe a fist maybe a fish the bird was diving or dying
  toward it before flying away

Because that was the closest we came to its long gray neck and
  darker wings its nest of sticks in the tree tops

MARY HAMILTON

Too proud to pity my own sad fall, I cried
put off my gown but let my petticoat be and tie
a napkin 'round my eyes, my death I would not . . .

For I tied her in my apron neat and set her out.

For I placed her in a *piner-pig* and swore
she was no babe of mine and would *ne'er*
make a maire of me, as though I were no Mary at all

but my own carrion crow, quick skilled thief
of egg and nestling and no sad cry from my sore side
rose in the night like pity and shame.

Once I was safe among the other Maries,
tending the Queen of all our names, when he offered
his high Stewart grace and seed.

He would be my knave. We were meant to be
and he courted me. Yes, the kitchen and stair.

Yes, the low cellar, *the worst of all*,
though on my knees I prayed that God
might deliver this Mary from pride and thrall,

from being the one Mary of four—his delight
and choosing.

And I would not put on my robes of black, and neither
my robes of brown, but I put on my glistering gold
and shone my way to Edinboro town.

She had opened blue eyes and a mouth
as purpled with need as a king.

She was bane and boon, bonny and wee
and our bitter weeping polished the halls
until *word was up to Madam the Queen.*

And there is a song in several versions.

Like a plea, let it stay and brother your sleep.
Let it thread your growing like prophecy
and stitch you to a sweet refrain.

Now lift the stylus and ease it down
toward the third black vinyl groove from silence,
be the haunted chamber of her sink or swim.

And sing of me in common rhyme and even stanzas:
*for last night the Queen had four Maries
and this night she'll have but three.*

He had a stranger's touch and a king's grammar.
He tasted like the sea.

I had borne a babe. Mr. Child records the tale
in several versions. *There was Mary Seaton
an' Mary Beaton an' Mary Charmichael an' me.*

FRONT PAGE

Finally it becomes too much: the mostly women
and children look of things, the smudge in the photo
where the town billows with God's wrath. In Genesis,
when Lot invites the mysterious visitors to his house
an angry mob gathers and he offers up his two
virgin daughters—but no one remembers that. We all
have our eyes trained on the pillar of salt
carved by wind into a woman whose name

does not register. If a neighbor had barged
into my childhood at dinnertime, his face and eyes
obscure behind black wool or soft plastic,
shouting in our language that we must take
what we can carry and clear out in ten minutes,
we might be shocked by the aim of his hate
the hard battalion of teeth as the harsh words
shot past but his name would not be found
in the family address book though the voice
might be familiar and his shoes from afternoons
I'd seen him polishing his motorcycle. And when

he brought his rifle butt against my father's lower skull
to emphasize his orders, my father thinking, *pogrom,
cossack*, it's not that I would want that suffering
or the forced march and exile, but how would you feel
if you couldn't get your mother into the picture
and didn't know if she would finally turn away
from her engagement with the middle distance
to look at him again, see the ooze and broken skin
beneath his right ear, finally speak, repeat
his crushed name, like an invocation. The soldier

in the next piece looks a lot like the man
he's taken prisoner and the dark excesses coursing
through his small intestine would smell precisely
like our own if we ever let the story sink in and turned

properly afraid. But the ink that grays everything I feel
that day, the reports of men marched into the woods,
of bodies systematically changed to damaged goods
becomes too much so I turn to p.13
for the human angle, and the story of Mustaf Hoti
who says he'll never touch his wife again.

If your true love turned to salt on the way to Zoar
would you lick her or keep walking, ask
what could be done, what could I do?

Everything done and spoken, touched and read,
each shifting tongue and still or moving body

burnishes our bits and particles or takes
some sheen away. Every word that has bitten in

or broken skin, all the books, sweat ribbons,
the uncanny uncelestial bodies in flight and retreat.

And yet to stay continuous and exactly the same,
or claim it, back in California summer upon summer

scrambling memory with landscape—
fundamental childheart in the waves at Big Sur beach

and later at nineteen, hiking switchback trails
toward sun-spent Echo Lake.

And then again these elevations of no forgiveness
for the uncertain foot, the sheer cliffs and brown

outcroppings, ice plants and cacti that scratch our calves,
the dry pine-heated air, complete and correspond

but don't quite, or do but cannot meet
some sheerer need for green limit and enclosure.

Otherwise, why not stay at home among cottonwoods,
high silvery grass, riffs of color that satisfy hunger

so thoroughly, we hardly see them? Wouldn't I
have continued to thrive among columbine,

this Indian paintbrush oranging the mountainside,
where all along the fire line scrub rises midday

to find the sky charcoaled to night, the moon scarlet.

Far above the malleable half-rib floater,
a sudden unexpected pain

skitters where the skin curve of the fifth rib
builds a parking lot

and the left breast rises toward moonish
areolar light.

A magnetic jolt? The deadly current
that electrifies the eel? And from my mouth

a cramped unnatural squeal or cry, as if I
were the only woman left

with two small breasts, a steady heart with two
varieties of song: beat

and beaten, hark and harkens, whole and holy.
Listen. The cricket cannot halt

his call. It owns him. Any regret
you hear is mine. He wraps himself around

the knot of that single note and shines
and when the shining stops, he's gone. (It's over.)

Two

DISLOCATION

Outside, sap rides the cellulose corridors
of deciduous trees with no good intentions
just science and a summer of flexible leaves:

flat receptive machines churning sugary food
from light and light and oxygen.

All winter they withhold what is best
and most astonishing and I thought I could follow suit
with no greenery to symbolize

my will-of-the-wisp, my ghost of a chance,
the promised end of promise.

But don't believe what you read
in a book by its cover.

In Southern California (where I grew up)
Summer's dress was brown.
Flowers bloomed in season and out.

Nothing moved but waves, nothing swooned
or withdrew into stasis.

Now a strange land myself, not the wild,
not the West, I know appearances can lie
down with the lamb and come in like a lion

or a soap opera fate, adark and amourning,
turning a new leaf season of dismay.

GHAZAL FOR THE FIRST DAY OF SPRING

Dreaming of fig trees that grow only here in Iraq
the minah cries out and every heart tears in Iraq.

Last night seven wedding parties drove down our street
tooting car horns and trumpets. O strange, false cheer in Iraq.

In my dream the Apache thunk-thunks at the windows
of our emptied-out rooms at Hotel Al Fanar in Iraq.

On a dusty boulevard, city workers plant trees.
On foot and in cars, their neighbors clear out of Iraq.

They surrendered from ditches but our road graders
buried alive old men and boys years ago in Iraq.

The Tigres-Euphrates runs brown with sewage and black
with petroleum soot. It's the air that we fear in Iraq.

It's true I have a slight fever, no appetite. I sleep
too much but this fear sickness is not rare in Iraq.

As the day's first missiles seek out their targets,
the muezzin calls the pious to prayer in Iraq.

And you, my friend, have you written a letter to mail
to loved ones if you die or disappear in Iraq?

CHILD'S PLAY

When I was Queen, the neighbor boy
sang *fermez la bouche* or *off with her head.*

The other was brave and pleasant to see but for two
distinct flaws, a large mole on her neck, on her left hand,

an extra finger, while I could not say what I was
or knew, where orifice or my shins were.

Chin, I once had opened against the sidewalk
and had closed with three dark stitches.

The open, where the pain like a lady-in-waiting,
like glass breaking easily under my fist.

Or the boy on the playground whose coat-of-arms
read *love of the rack and the screw.*

Already on her knees with sorry she replied,
I have heard the executioner . . . and I have a little neck.

For they could be kicked, shins could, with a vow
or pledge and godspeed in the deliverance.

Of course she knew what hands were for, that it was easy
to mistake the ardor of love for something ominous.

And didn't we pray to end our days among walls and nuns,
keep our darkness inside where it could harm us.

The promised end enough to bring on the small-
death adagio of want and dread.

At the trial, her lover swooned, and was carried from the room before her raised face spoke from the underside of blindfold:

For a gentler nor a more merciful prince was there never
and to me he was ever a good, a gentle and sovereign lord.

Pressure is the ludic god: the blood vessels
fill and celebrate, *Selah*. Oh I admit

I like it best when the unslippered fingertip
totters between the Judas kiss and the actual

besotted song. Then the palm fronds sway
and every whale is the right one. But in the final

episode, when he rolled the condom
down with ease and blind efficiency,

I climbed on to do what I was there for,
what many a girl might try. And who

is to blame, the soul, or the tongue that curls for brine
and curve of bicep, the belief that if part of him

were inside me, the spirit wasn't far
behind. I, we were making hay, my full name

sprawled across the screen right on top
of his. Though he linked his hands behind

his neck like a convict being moved from bus
to prison, like a person doing sit-ups

and we only touched through clouded latex,
a rosy-fingered dawn was rising just outside

my point of view, and while the placards insisted
in bold red *the end is near*, in my basket heart

and sundry flesh I wanted more, I didn't care.

Long Division

Cell wall, smooth membrane, nucleus
and spindle. The sell, switch and swindle.
The least excuse and leap of faith blind
journey toward the emptied trees
that branch indifference and leafless gold relief.

The *mittleschmertz*. The randy oocyte
site of troubles and vast vast difference.
The stirrup and speculum. Another chance
and promise beneath the cool conductive
gel of compromise. The pointing arrow
pointing out an unformed pounding wish.

A list of things in me he finds untenable,
miser of my misery, man who holds
his head and sighs *you ruin my life.*

The narrow miss *out out damn spot*
of blood. The man machined who murmurs
now count back from ten and squeeze . . . .
We finish or unbegin what ends before
the problem's solved but long after
the long remainder that is carried.

What sentence can be executed to lay to rest
with a comfortable phrase or clarify
this ordered rage, past shame and long past grace—.

"I think he got what he wanted," Jay Sawyer added.
"Without saying a word, he got the final word."

"O monstrous! monstrous!"
—*Othello*

Proem

Though we did not lose a loved one, we will probably wear
our Sunday clothes.

I was thinking about my son and leaned his picture
up against the window, glad a country can make an example
like a full stop at the end of a sentence
that preserves the freedom.

There were many days we thought we would not again
experience joy, for in our hearts
it will always be April in Oklahoma.

Warden

He has stepped into the chamber and sat down
at our table—his final hours spent, his chosen
final meal consumed—and positioned himself

so we may apply restraint, then sodium pentothal,
which causes sleep, pancuronium bromide, which stops
the breath, and potassium chloride, which keeps the heart

from beating and puts to death at thirty-three
at local time, the first to die by step-by-step
"efficient and humane" procedures.

Witness

At 7:10 his skin and lips turned pale and strange,
as he filled his cheeks with air and seemed
to ration his remaining.

I saw deep breaths, a fluttery breath. His gulping
cheeks did swallow and puff, I saw that twice,
his chest moving, his body spasming
as he let go—defiant to the end.

His eye was almost watery with trying to resist,
staring at the ceiling seeming proud as he looked us
eye to eye to stare us down, trying to take charge
and looking proud of what had happened.

His eye was blinking open closed.
His eye unblinking seemed coal black.
His totally expressionless blank stare told
that if he could he'd do it again.

Yet in the end, I felt he was afraid,
and I think I did see the face of evil
with my own face right up against the window
and his glare turned to the video camera over his head

like he was staring into our souls
and the devil was inside looking through me.

Official Statement

This morning carried the severest sentence, the gravest crime, so that every living person can rest in knowledge of a reckoning, of final punishment that cannot alone bring peace, recover loss or balance scales, and is not meant to do so, for the case was proved and the verdict calmly reached and under law the matter is concluded.

We have seen the good that overcomes evil in the rescuers who saved and suffered the victims, a community grieved and held close, the work of detectives, marshals and police and in the courts where due process ruled.

With all eyes on Terre Haute today we make it as positive as possible, having gathered no joy and not asking for the execution to be here, but we are pleased to have the federal penitentiary as partner and the people who come, for the first and last time, can go away with a feeling of what our city is really like, the victims given not vengeance but justice, and one young man the fate he chose himself, and killing as part of the healing.

Like a simple math of exchange and addition,
replacing 'a' with 'i,' and adding hard 'c' to get nothing,
death inspires the atmosphere and keeps hounds,

running the soft pink eraser back toward the margin
and over their names: Verhoeven's, Vespucci's, Nelson's
McClear's—cave-dwelling, rice-eating, bushy-tailed cloud—

all kin to the wily and wild brown *Rattus norvegicus*
whose high-pitched skittering subways the rails
at the edges of dream and brings home our disease.

Beside this tree, under these low and fallen
they preyed and foraged, clawed to injury, sniffed
and sprayed. Upon the fruited, along the vernal

and desolate streams, we mistook good fortune
for feed and a ride. Now are we venial and wear the willow,
for this morning the newspapers say the last of the last

true Emperor rats has surrendered his electorate
of fleas to a body impolitic, gristle and fur.

LESSON

Temple Bar, Dublin

We are in the dark and walk
a quiet enough empty city street

when footsteps hurry sudden from behind
and from nowhere what cannot be

is on us with his pocketknife pressed up
against your *fucking American* gullet

and your hands no longer empty push
against his arms that do what cannot be

as in slow motion. Standing next door
to your brain, I saw your scalp as pale as death

beneath your hair's close crop, the carotid artery's
pulse of blood. *Run* you screeched and suddenly

the street was moving, *Help* was pealing
from my lips. He was so slight—feet lifted

from the ground as you stood up to shake
him off. In Kilmainham gaol we saw the yard

where Plunkett and the others were grimly
blindfolded and shot. *I'll fucking kill*

you as he ran off. Glancing through the single
window slots into the whitewashed cells

I tried to think about his life but couldn't
help the litany that rose instead:

robbers thugs bandits fingersmiths crooks
murderers blackguards cutthroats thieves.

33

CENTO: LAST WORDS

Monsieur, I beg your pardon.
I love you. I'd like to thank
my family for loving me.
Thank you for the change
in my life. You have given me,
the love and closeness, my family,
my beautiful girl. Thank you
for using me though I owe society
nothing. The Lord is going to get
another one. Yes, I'm going face
to face with Jesus now and I
will see you when you get there.
For you can be a king or a street
sweeper, but everyone dances
with the Grim Reaper. Make no mistake.
I will wait for you, though I am innocent,
innocent, innocent, and something
very wrong is taking place. I don't hold
any grudges. Such is life and today
is a good day to die. So the heart be right,
it is no matter which way the head lies.
Take a step forward. Shoot straight
and don't make a mess. It will be easier
that way. Lock and load. Let's do it.
Beam me up, I'm on my way.
Get the ride started. I'm ready to go.
Adios. I guess no one is going to call.
I killed a man, O God forgive me,
I killed a man. O Jesu Maria!
Have mercy on my soul.

LAMENT

A person dies and does not do the dishes
or hear the soap-and-water song
that grants a cleansing task with clear-cut goals
and steam to keep the cold does not at bay

A person dies and does not do and dishes
might pile up beside the sink where they will keep
until the morning that does not rise but breaks

A person who does not do his dishes dies
and someone else must find the cake and icing smear
and know his final meal was tasted undigested
his last does not blue night on the nod

A person dies and does not do before he never answers
calls again or sleeps and breathes or ventures
the can of worms that might but does not open

A person does not nor morning nor sun nor heat
return to comfort those who arrive where he does not
to fold wash and neatly pack his things away

THREE

Unholy 14

Wallop my ticker, triple-threat man with a plan; so far
you just diddle, pant, burnish and look to fix my wagon;
that I may get off the ground, make me see daylight
and wind up your best shot to cold-cock, knuckle, drill,
whale and revolutionize my ass. I, like a Baghdad overrun
by troops, break my balls to give you access, but O,
I just can't get no satisfaction. Brains, your main man on my street
should lifeguard me but he's in the hole and has no guts
or loyalty. And sure you are my *Ichiban* and would I were
all that, but your all-time least favorite son has got me
on my hands and knees. Unmarry me, unhook the strap
or smithereen that fastener once more; squeeze me tight,
wall me in, for I, unless you take me prisoner won't ever make
parole; won't ever be immaculate unless you bang my bones.

Contrarious Passions in a Love

You paddle out in the sleek green canoe
to row back to shore, meander with care

and rush without heed. You want to unnest
but not scare, put back and frighten,

catch sight of the bird as if natural life
and uncanny death depend on it,

requiring nothing. The lake is an opaque
opalescence, moving somewhere perfectly still,

that *holds you not, yet can you scape no wise*—
fed by sound and starved into silence.

Sometimes you dive in to rise up
from the sky, surrender and take prisoners

in the horizontal rhythm, the vertical
anomaly of faith and falseness. The monster

at its core lies quiet as shallowed angels
arise and cry out, arise and bark.

Between strokes and during them, a name
calls you back to send you packing.

You fear and hope, you burn, and freeze,
the answer swimming also, the question

drowning on shore. But the lessons that stick
are absorbed by flesh and repelled by the mind,

and the swimmer's hand caught your jaw
hard as he passed, *though nought you have*

and all the world you seize, as if sleeping awake,
the dream done, the hour's early beginning.

Two Envelopes

She likes to think of him at seventeen,
leaning toward the cards that make a figure
on the bedroom floor, his privacy intact, unbroken,
clean hair falling darkly falling past his shoulder
past his eye, and wonders what took flight there
before philosophy and the problem of two
envelopes, the proof that always aims at absolute.

As he contemplates—is it the Fool, the Six
of Swords foretelling flight and arduous journey—
she wants him nervous full of hope, his fingers
damp, wants the burning question to burn

for some Melanie of miniskirt and fishnet high-wedge
platform shoes and thigh, and wants him to take heart
and have one, urgencies that get the better of him
like this high delightful howl that wrenches from his lungs—.

It is what she lives for, that sound of boy, caterwaul
that spurns the closed unhappy fist unfree beneath his ribs:
it knocks and pounds but cannot release cannot.

ORNITHOLOGY II

He wants to know what kind of bird
has built a nest in the tree
beside my window but I'm tired of diligence
and tireless activity, the indifferent
beak, the singer everyone has heard.
That mechanical racket has terrorized the crows—
now they're on the run or wing
to scour another grassy patch. Song
is a secondary sex character
generally restricted to the male
but all birds have a calling, a heart
in hiding, even those black hangers-on
that gather like menace
wherever the ground-life flowers.
Don't expect them to regulate
mosquito populations, sing full-
or half-hearted of joy illimited.
Open their gullets and find a few bees,
many grasshoppers, streaks of blood
and meat in the lucky ones, extended
wings. As common as the breeze
that carries death in our direction,
they seem one note, but the guidebook praises
their extensive vocabulary: *caw*,
a hundred subtle variations. Call them
what you will, what you would never
in a million years, they have a sense
of decency, flying off as we
come round the bend and that small innocent
whose steely chatter taunts and obsesses
is an Eastern Kingbird. Its Latin name,
I looked it up, is *Tyrannus tyrannus*.

The Unsent and Unselected Letters

> "If a woman dreams of African scenes, her journeys
> will prove lonesome, devoid of pleasure or profit."
> —*The Dictionary of Dreams*
> Gustavus Hindman Miller, 1909

Maasai Mara

As far away as I have come, I am here and you are
the argument in wheel-long hours of gazing landscape,
and they are many in this out-the-window moving

false diversion. Nothing, not the infamous acacia
pride of lions resting in its shade, not the kill that's slain
and splayed dispatched four days now, maggot ridden,

not hartebeest nor wildebeest, nor the life-paired
dikdik can distract the drone that hovers close and pulls
away its monotonous crop duster song and fright.

I wanted strange escape, not you in the bottom slide
of every thought and view, or this fear it could be syphilis
that makes me limp, not this mania to record and list, invent

the sight of bird that will not focus into view,
while all around me automatic cameras click
and whir, for we are on the trail now of the leopard.

Arboreal, nocturnal, difficult to spot, we all believe
we see his dead antelope up a tree, so point our lenses
out an open window and we shoot.

Ngong Hills

Would you love the garden crammed with three banana trees, the rose and other flowering sticky leaves, the ruby, white and orange overflows of bougainvillea lush on lush—.

Don't you have a taste for animosity, metallurgy and it's true that every house and bungalow has bars on windows, bars on doors, that almost everyone I've met has been accosted, car-jacked, raped or robbed at gun point, shut inside the car boot, burglarized in the night as they slept.

Restless, half-unmade I left the compound Saturday and found myself the sole *wazungu* walking the Containment Road to Westlands against your better judgment. How many drivers pulled alongside to save me from folly or pulled their hat brims low or looked away in the shops as I bargained like a dealer?

In Karen the museum had the boots Streep wore, a linen jacket stained by Redford's shoulders but the writing table seemed to be authentic. Sometimes I cannot think or sleep straight through another night, another dream of mood and speech that cannot confess there is no danger. In one you would not read between small rages that I beat against your chest or end the foolishness that made me plead and wheedle when you walked away from my rebuff.

The compound locks us in the flowering safety of the aid we bring. Like you, the Kenyans hurry the way they go and pay me no attention. As Blixen wrote in a letter she never posted, *We could not know and could not imagine the dangers that they fear from our hands.*

Lead Apron

I remember the accident: the invisible wire strung
across the bikepath, the shock of helmet crash,

then me, resting in the August weeds with bicycles swooning
in the background, my skin going black

where the wire had done its business.

Later in Emergency, I accepted the lead apron
as if I already knew: no false alarm, a many
hearted cell was flowering.

It seems that Karen too had all the signs
and knew them. The coded wire Fitzpatten sent,

like everything, brings you here to me, unbearable,
unbidden (my response has never

been recovered): *Strongly urge you cancel
Daniel's visit STOP I should welcome him*

if I could offer partnership. But is impossible STOP.

I keep it closed but the landscape presses in like a child
holding out a photo of the life

we have rescued from ruin, or a voice repeating lessons
in another room, *aye, iii, eye, oh you, oh you,*

vows, from the alphabet of the haunted.

Mt Kenya

It was the hardest task though none of us carried our weight
and I made promises. Above all you need a warm bag,

a balaclava or woolly hat, an emergency
foil blanket. To ascend the scree takes three hours

deep breaths and steady climbing, though the porters,
whose names I tried to learn—Joseph, Moses, Isaac,

Wilson, Joseph, Paul, and Cyrus—raced ahead
their blood thin and rich with oxygen-gleaning cells,

thin and vulnerable. Near the top we waited on a ledge
for dawn to break and I was almost there and almost

felt the cold and sudden height, the above all place
of looking down toward sea and plain, and very small

the villagers or animals teeming with where to get to.
On New Years, Moses says, two hundred Kisumu Girl Guides

will reach the summit. CDC data suggests that in ten years,
one in four of those girls—how to say it—will be gone, will be dead.

Effects of altitude include nausea,
slurred speech and headaches and I blame my heart

too small and overzealous, though I held a hand to stop
the dizziness, though I placed my foot,

as I tired and winded, not to slip or cave in,
and had read a book to memorize statistics and the wariness:

It took 800,000 years to smooth the angled skull
and truncated face of *Homo erectus* to *Homo sapiens*,

to gain 400 ccs in the cranial room, and during the 1920s
the black rhinoceros was poached almost to extinction.

Everyone I've met has an uncle, cousin, friend,
a boss, and I think it's true, what Joseph said as we descended

We do not think of you, that you can ever forget us.

If I know a song of Africa, of the new moon lying on her back,
of ploughs in fields, and the sweaty faces of the coffee-pickers,
does Africa know a song of me?

Spirit Turn

Born with every egg tucked neatly
in her side, a woman might find
our lives are Swiss, so still, so cool,

though she knows it is never too early
or late to begin, and her cervix feels firm
and closed and dry, though she hums

in her fine electrical skin, and prays
that the ready ones unglue and fly
where the Yew trees blow like hydra.

I was like her and better than her, neater
at crewel, swifter at charting my infertile
phases. I placed a pillow underneath

my hips, marked the chart each time
we tried, and let my feelings range
from mild ache to true discomfort.

They say you die from the cry
as roots pull from the earth, but I wrested
my mandrake, and sweated through six

different changes of shirt. I cut five
fresh henbane leaves, found three Marias,
a Pedro, and a Juan. But with my blood

that turns wine and stills bees in their hives
when I was dead, my spirit turned.
Each name that made a bed of my tongue

dissolved in the frame and the busy of lives
and the clocks all chimed too late, too fine.
O, when I was dead, my spirit turned

where the Yew trees blow like hydra,
and each name that made a bed of my tongue
yearned to beat small wings of flame

but dissolved in the frame and the busy of lives.

Her Best

A swallow flies between the eaves beside my window
and a shallow portion of the lawn
where worms strive—

with much swooping off and descending,
much back and forth
and forth again.

Something glitters in her yellow beak,
and with each approach her wings splay out, the smaller
fingered tail-feathers spreading too

as she applies the brakes. A pause,
a death, then gratitude or need
begins its thin

incessant plea. It rises from the throat,
a pink translucent skull
and tufts of down,

an undivided heart, blinking lantern-like
beneath a clutch of ribs that I can only imagine.
And the mother bird,

who surely does her best, flies off long before
the squawking ends (though it does end)
and is gone

much longer than I expected.

See the ball of the thumb, flat and withered
or choose a word to pin it to the page.

Only the buried question mark, a curled
vestigial ear, can hear my fingers sad caress.

He's disappeared to smooth involuntary sheets
that make the lungs contract, expand, contract,

to breath and breathing, more or less a fund of wisdom
splintered from inside. Ganglia have stopped

transmitting heat and pain and cold and fear—
each message to the spine returns unwrapped,

unheeded. When what has hidden seeks
to fracture voice, *your hair smells nice,*

this sudden body, not mine and nothing left,
takes heart into custody and the hatchet up again.

LETTER FROM A HAUNTED ROOM

Dear K., there's a mosquito stain
between the pages of your book, a streak
of platelets beside my index finger.
The broken microscopic cells have escaped
the hurly-burly of the wide aorta, the stark
unholy flow through veins and tubules.
Don't get me wrong. I don't mistake
anatomy for emotion. My heart is meat
and gristle, like Artaud's: a simple
pump, it never falters. If I weep
it's for the rocking chair, three knocks
embedded in the nursery wall.
On one window, I found instructions:
"Here, no cares invade, all sorrows
cease" in almost perfect iambs.
Forgive me. I tried to keep them
"far outside" but they marched right up
to my room. All month they've been waving
tenuous arms. Have you seen them?
What could I do but let them in
and let them rest in your favorite chair. Soon
they'll disappear or I will. In the after-
noons (do you remember?) light falls
or spills, spills or falls through the amber
stained-glass windows. It lifts my spirits
but I'm still waiting for you to appear
at the edge of my bed with a message. Think
of the ruins I could have traveled to
by now, think of the days I've wasted
lying on the pink divan, a stand of hawthorns
blocking my view of the rose garden,
my American Beauty, already fully blown.

8ᵗʰ & Pine, 4/23, 24 Hour Store, you wore blue eye
shadow, walked in my direction, looking right
at me: 5'8", brown hair, brown eyes, black leather
jacket, humming some aria underneath your bated
breath—something I recognized but cannot put
my finger on. Please call. ASAP. I saw you on the 57
Winston, Thursday, 5/3 or 4. You, reading *How to Read
a Poem*, glanced up & it just clicked but you got off
at Cooper St. without a glance. I tried to follow.
Lost you. Sorry if I blew it. Call before 5 or after midnight
or anytime. Billy's Bar, St. Paddy's Day. You,
at one end, dark long hair & boots. I'm the guy
with three drunk friends & bedroom eyes.
Your boyfriend is a loser. His haircut looks like shit.
Meet me there any Sunday. I'll buy. I saw you walk
your chocolate lab on Broadway, Thursday,
3 A.M. You shrugged I think & then said "hi" or "hey"
or maybe "help." I wore a pink turtleneck, braids.
I think we knew each other in another life. We need
to talk. I saw you wasting time & saw your
desperation, etc., at the bus stop dressed in yellow
fur & yellow light & on the train I saw you talking
to the window in a brown & orange windbreaker,
polishing your nails a dusky mauve. I saw you, saw
your ambiance, your icicles & slow smile
pasted on a subway ad. On the sidewalk
you were pedaling rapidly away despite my shouts
& pleading. In my mind I saw you glancing
toward my voice & in my dream weren't you
pulling off my underwear & screaming *Cadillac*
or some French word I do not know. I think we have
a lot in common. Please write this number down & call.

FOUR

And then arrive from the other side where *she*
is born, not birthed but made, traced and cut

from female traits, or the row of books
that underlined a library life, ready to burn

transform her all along the Little, the Ugly
and Steadfast Tin nerves. From Matchgirl,

Mermaid, Duckling, Soldier, she came,
no Catcher in Rye, no Lord of Flies but Lisa,

Bright and Dark to a Never Promised Rose
Garden of *no*, to ballads of pure-hearts

left to sink or swim far from the bonny
shore. In her sorrow and woe, she intoned

Will There Really Be a Morning and flew Up
the Down Staircase toward a Patch of Blue,

not blind but a Sybil setting fire in the Jar
and the Bell with So Much to Tell You.

Then Suddenly Last Summer, Whatever
Happened to Baby Jane, she lost her appetite

for riding Eden Express, or searching Dibs:
In Search of Self, for David and Lisa.

Long sentences and actual verbs that *strung,
leapt, bouldered, paced* would unleave her,

Golden, Notebooked, darkening her fingertips
run along strings of words and To the Lighthouse.

BLUE PLASTIC TARP

Because this is Southern California and the plants of childhood
are succulent, dandelion,
camellias in constant scentless bloom,

it could be October, it could be May.

The girl doesn't know of the family of frogs spawning
in what they believe is the ancestral pond,
but she is singing to something,

tracing a path from walnut to mulberry to lemon and back.

Her mother is gone but not to the usual places
in suburbia and this is what needs
to be made sense of (the heart and the crux),

what she, years later, will fail to discern in the break, the caesura.

The sun in the lemon tree and the black plums
that stain the pavement warms my shoulderblades
through the light checkered fabric of memory.

In *Why Has Bodhi-Dharma Left for the East?*
the master, the orphaned boy and apprentice
were one, and all or each had left his mother blind

in an unnamed Korean city.

At the end, or near it, the apprentice disappears
into enlightenment and the orphan burns
the master's robes. (The master burns as well
on a pyre fired by sticks, dead leaves and gasoline.)

Each was devising a way to slip sideways
through the needle's eye, to thread the whirlwind.
One answer to the Koan, *cypress tree in the garden,*

is nothing but a high-class riddle to me—
though "I" am only what evades the bar: the few, the least
perilous aches or ecstasies, small gifts that return

from the blank screen or ignite it and sing *I am, I am*:

waiting in the backyard at dusk, the front, the back
the sliding glass all locked against me; someone at fault
or else no one

would yell and yell that way.

Maybe it's not that day but one near by and the father
never sat like patience at the empty kitchen table—
"Emergency" a word remembered from TV, learned later.

Maybe the mother had always gone and this
is what appears to mark it, percolating from below the plastic tarp
like a dream she meant to keep.

Asked if he is sad about the mother he has never known,
the orphan says, "How can I be sad,
since I don't remember" but the rock he throws wounds

a starling's mate and the widowed cry
haunts and terrifies until the orphan falls or leaps
from the wooded cliff to a shallow pool below.

For a long time, the camera shows us a panic splash
of arms and legs while not far off
the rocky shore absorbs the white calm of afternoon.

Which scene does the boy retain?

The fall, the struggle or later when he wakes damp and cold
or later still when he sleeps again and dreams
of wet hair and a low moan and whatever lies hidden

underneath the heavy soaked-through fabric of her dress.

And the girl, remember her, for years the only part she'll know
is true is the chemical light of evening
and the parking lot where they went to fetch her,

she'll recall a bright cotton dress, the front seat
suddenly full again.

HER WHITE-WORKED SAMPLER

Worked in linen thread on fine white linen,
a demanding form of fancy cutwork, not lace

but delicate as a baby's hand, she marked
her upper and lower cases, stitched herself

in rhyme and alphabet to keep within compass,
avoid the mischief Satan makes for idle hands.

Her fingers took eagerly to the whip,
the flame, the French knot and buttonhole.

But everything she knew of love was said in cross:

This strangler wrought with so much caribou
Adorned with commas rich and fair

My little frog let it impart a mortal lesion to thy heaven.

FALSE REPRIEVE

One day my mother slips at the entrance
to the Safeway, an on the floor, down

to the bone shattering that finds her unhinged
where the true blue veins of business branch

and twist. And with a snap, a crunch
and resounding moan a four-year silence

breaks open—

as if each unbegun conversation, all the words
and phrases withheld or put aside

in pursuit of the intractable eye turned inward
had pooled there like heat,

simmering the marrow, making newly minted
RBCs and platelets jump and flail.

It's not hard to imagine with a scientific
vocabulary or a sentimental habit of mind:

that morning they were at the table, one facing north,
the other tuned to the hypothetical ocean.

Then it's the afterward he went through
to collect her without cruelty and didn't yell,

after the doctor had explained she'd need a steel pin
(stainless) and they were both on the line

saying *What? What? It's fine, she's fine*, giddy
with the long avoided: two voices sounding

in their living room—

And why am I surprised, the fractured
always near: the ocean one block from anywhere

with its littoral zone and replicate waves,
and aren't her bones just as delicate as mine?

Nothing resolves when I squint
at the pale blue horizon the next day.

Nothing revolves but the phonograph
left on the moon. Let the room be absolved

of all that remains unspoken
and the children returned to the family ruse.

The second red welt appeared,
not a wound this time but a window
to black liquid roiling underneath,
a view not out but in and hard
to the touch too sensitive
inflamed and she thought of Dickinson
whose soul had bandaged moments
and Teresa of Ávila, her palsied heart and fainting
fit passion or speech to God. *Heal thyself,*
she thought Christ said that and Lazarus,
good as new after four days
without a breath or oxygen-rich heartbeat:
no stench, no maggots, all because of faith.
The surgeon offered seven shots of Novocain,
a scalpel. *Don't scratch a bite*
until it bleeds. Don't rub up against
or abut. She tried to believe
pushing the bandage into the wound at night,
pulling out dead tissue in the morning.
What's eating you, someone asked
and her left leg answered with authority:
the brown recluse is never lethal
but its sting can bring decay
to an otherwise healthy limb.
Recently scientists have confirmed
that the gut has a mind of its own
as ancient and cold-blooded as a lizard.
Soon they'll discover that every cell
has a story and a prayer. If anything
you say can and will be held against you,
why not let the body have its day?
One doctor drew a ring around
the bright pink cellulitis. One asked her
to talk about her dreams the flesh repeats

and reproduces: she soaked through
twelve rolls of gauze and limped
for forty-seven days. Her body,
her heresy, a ghastly unbecoming.

NATURAL PROCESSES

For two months, I've been the bowl
and what overspills the brim,
set off kilter by a random phrase

or set of notes, the cricket's weary
echo of my own query: *how could you?*
how could you? In seven years the slick

epithelial cells that line my throat
will be replaced. Completely different
corpuscles will haul the poison

carbon dioxide to my lungs
to be exhaled, a transfer of gasses
so quick no one notices. But the body

is a miracle: the DNA will replicate
the same unhappy sequence and like the snake
who leaves its old self in the grass,

I'll slough away this skin that could not
satisfy or keep him. Already the cells'
engines are at work and with millions

of chromosomes lining up
and dividing, I'll soon be someone
else, as familiar and strange

as the farm hand on that late train
heading south who pressed his leg
against mine as he slept. I woke

to his nicotine breath, and grew
so accustomed to the rhythm
and the rough stubbled folds

below his chin, when he rose
to de-train in Charlottesville
I almost kissed him. A friend of mine

says ordinary tears are mostly salt
and water. Tears of grief are full
of protein. With a microscope,

you can see the disappointment
broken down into carbon chains
and sulfides. I've been undone

by chemistry and natural processes
and next week when a doctor
numbs the mole between my shoulder

blades and removes it with a scalpel,
I'll have saved myself for the stranger
who will kiss that scar with awe.

Meteor Shower

Any eye can see the field, frozen hard and furrowed
in straight lines to a horizon of winter deep November

and for the ones on the ground there is no comfort but the sky
is paramount, is fireball and grazer, white flare and red tinge

with tails all gesturing back to the heart of the radiant.

How rich to be returned to the storm not shower, given
back to the almost illegal blue black panel of the mind's eye

that cannot unblink fast enough, where again stars fall like rain
or rain like potsherds or do not fall but arrive on fire, burning

at several thousand degrees through the clean upper atmosphere,
blazing as the earth collides with the dust trail ribbon of debris

painted by the comet's tail one hundred and more years ago.

This is the magnitude of night, aligned and reordered
and we are in the picture too, flat on our backs

or tilted toward the backwards question mark of Leo, for once
and always in the bone chill and awe as the animal spirit

nuzzles a hand or barks and leaps up at a sky that is falling.

ESCAPE THE NO WISDOM OF

Experience what is traditionally described as the fruit of *maitri*—
   playfulness.

Something that happens as a result of working with precision and
   the gentle

Common misunderstanding among all human beings who have
   ever been born on earth that the best way to live is to try to
   avoid pain and just try to get comfortable won't

Alleviate human misery at a personal and global level.

Part of the technique is that when you realize you've been
   thinking, you say to yourself "thinking."

Emotions that we have right now, the negativity and the positivity,
   are what we actually need for

The end of the out breath.

He talks about the four kinds of horses: the excellent horse, the
   good horse, the poor horse, and the really bad horse as if at the

End of each day, someone were to play a video of you back to
   yourself,

Never encouraged to see clearly what is, with gentleness, more

Open-hearted than any of that.

What will make us complete, sane, grown-up people and what—if
    we are too involved in it—will keep us children forever

I couldn't visualize.

Stomach and shoulders and body and that you can be softer with
    the out breath and more sympathetic with the labeling

Doesn't mean getting rid of anything,

Or her.

Misunderstanding our daily lives that we all share, something that
    can be turned around, corrected and seen through, as if we
    were in a dark room and someone showed us where the light
    switch was, that

Other people are terrible, and I'm right to be so angry all the time,

Fully awake and alive, fully human.

Second Wind

Late in the first year and twenty-first
century, no starling or sparrow

in hand and nest, no murmuration
or ruinous host, no dissimulation of bird

could undo what she saw in the blue,
for it opened her *vox humana*

and she caught in that net on the same
day and same month with five years of difference.

And ever since, with his deeper blue
plucked accompaniment, his more than

enough more, she was always with
her thoughts and never bored, alongside

his long and small sometimes in motion
always moving muscle and skin.

Along too for the yard work and jump
seat ride, a gamble never so smooth

or sure, with no phrase for the way
he put grassblade to lips, pressing thumbs

to the million fine hair swaying filaments
unstrung at the center of song.

The italicized lines in "Hands and Psalms" are borrowed from the *Antioch Guide to Dating*.

Information in "My Sole Genealogy" about the history of the Sewell family name is taken from several different web sites including the "Sewell/Sewall Family Records" page, "The Sole Society" page and "Robert Sewell's Genealogy Pages."

In "Seizure," the information about earthquakes was culled from Philip L. Fradkin's *Magnitude Eight: Earthquakes and Life Along the San Andreas Fault* and from the San Francisco Planetarium's web site.

"Name Withheld" describes two incidents. One is a late-night bike ride through Central Park during the summer of 1997. The other is an incident that occurred in broad daylight during the same summer when a group of women were accosted, stripped, and videotaped. Portions of the confiscated videotapes were later aired on television as part of the news coverage.

"Mary Hamilton" is a response to the fifteenth-century ballad, "Mary Hamilton," Child No. 173, which exists in at least two versions.

"Ghazal for the First Day of Spring" is based on the reports and diary entries of peace workers living in Iraq during the Spring of 2003.

Most italicized phrases in "Child's Play" are from Anne Boleyn's letters, or records of her speeches. The final lines of the poem are her final words. I have also borrowed from Sir Thomas Wyatt's "Whoso List to Hunt" (his translation of Petrarch's Sonnet 104) and from Sylvia Plath's poem "Daddy."

"Master of My Fate" is composed entirely of statements made by witnesses, news commentators, and local and national government officials on the day of Timothy McVeigh's execution, as reported by ABC, CNN, *The Guardian*, Court TV, and other news sources. The title is a line from William Ernest Henley's poem "Invictus," which McVeigh presented as his "last words."

"Cento: Last Words" compiles the final statements of many different people who have been executed, including Marie Antoinette, Karla Faye Tucker, Harry Harbord "Breaker" Morant, Gary Gilmore, and Sir Walter Raleigh.

"Unholy 14" is after John Donne.

Italicized lines and the title of "Contrarious Passions in a Love" are borrowed from Sir Thomas Wyatt's poem "Descriptions of the Contrarious Passions in a Lover."

Phrases included in "Ornithology II" are borrowed from poems by W. B. Yeats, Robert Frost, Gerard Manley Hopkins, Thomas Hardy, and Wallace Stevens.

Italicized lines in "The Unsent and Unselected Letters" are borrowed from Isak Dinesen's *Out of Africa* and from telegrams reproduced in Judith Thurman's biography of Dinesen.

Italicized lines in "Spirit Turn" are borrowed from poems by Emily Dickinson, Christina Rossetti, Sylvia Plath, and Anne Sexton.

"Meteor Shower" is based on a painting by Sarah McEneaney.

"Escape the No Wisdom Of" is an acrostic based on the first chapter of Pema Chodron's *The Wisdom of No Escape*. The reordering of the words in the title is followed in the poem.

Lisa Sewell is the author of *The Way Out* (Alice James Books). She has received grants and awards from the National Endowment for the Arts, the Leeway Foundation, the Pennsylvania Council for the Arts, and the Fine Arts Work Center in Provincetown. With Claudia Rankine, she is co-editor of *American Poets in the 21st Century: The New Poetics* (Wesleyan University Press). She teaches at Villanova University and lives in Philadelphia.